KEYS TO A Fruitful Life

PETER ADEGBIE

"This is to my Father's glory, that you bear much fruit,

showing yourselves to be my disciples"
John 15:8(NIV)

First, this book is Not a call to pharisaic morality and religion. God's desire and expectation from your life as a return on His investment is 'MUCH FRUIT', not just fruit or more fruit. Your fruitfulness honours God-Jesus Christ could report back to God-*"I have glorified thee…"* **John 17:14** and so must we because as Christ is so are we in this world-1John4:17.

However, just as in the natural, fruits do not just happen; you need the keys to unlock fruitfulness. I believe that this is the reason why this book has been divinely inspired and brought your way by divine providence.

Keys to a Fruitful Life is a MUST read for a life that is super abundant in quality and quantity brimming with fruit to the glory of God the Father.

Theodora Adegbie LLM, BL
CEO, E-Lawconsults, UK

Keys to a Fruitful Life will make you vigorous, holy, strong, a shining light filled with perfect love and Christ like maturity.

Tochi Okpara, MPharm

KEYS TO A FRUITFUL LIFE

COPYRIGHT (C) 2015

BY

PETER ADEGBIE

ISBN 978-1-911109-02-0

Published in the United Kingdom by
GOLDEN POT MEDIA

Cover Design and Page Layout

KENTEBA KREATIONS
www.kentebakreations.com

All rights preserved. No portion of this book may be used without the written permission of the publisher, with the exception of brief excerpts in magazines, articles, reviews, etc.

For further information or permission, address:
GOLDEN POT MEDIA
MICC
CORNHILL ROAD
SOUTHWICK
SSUNDERLAND, SR5 1RU
TYNE AND WEAR
UNITED KINGDOM
E-mail: adegbiepk@yahoo.com
Websites: www.goldenpotmedia.com
www.scli.org.uk

All scripture quotations are from the New International version of the Bible except otherwise stated.

DEDICATION

To Theodora, Daniel and Deborah-Divine who enrich my life, with the prayer that like Joseph, Daniel and Apostle Paul they will live a life of fruitfulness to God and mankind.

To all the Maximum Impact Christian Center and Chapel of Light family worldwide, with the prayer that together we can make a difference in the world as agents of change for Jesus Christ being fruitful in every good work.

CONTENTS

DEDICATION   7

INTRODUCTION   11

CHAPTER ONE
FOUNDATION FOR FRUITFULNESS   17

CHAPTER TWO
CHARACTERISTICS OF FRUITFULNESS   29

CHAPTER THREE
RELEASING GOD'S SEED OF FRUITFULNESS IN YOU   53

INTRODUCTION

Crackle of twigs and leaves
Litter the tree of righteousness
Branches hang hopefully
In the whistle of a windy day
Leaves sway without a care
Sudden rumbling thunder
Crack shots of lightening
Then clouds, unwraps blankets
Of sky, squeezing out
Droplets of fruitfulness
Trees beam and smiles
Again, it's time for fruitfulness
To drink in the heavenly delight
And present a blossom

To the king of righteousness

THIS BOOK is about fruitfulness; the revelation of God's will for you. Your dry season is over. It's time for your life to blossom.
'And God blessed them, and God said unto them, "Be fruitful, and multiply, and replenish the earth,"'

The same God who said "Let there be light" and 'there was light,' now declares "be fruitful and multiply." This divine utterance is for every realm of man's existence. As you study this book, I pray that covenant of fruitfulness shall become yours in Jesus' mighty name. Amen.

'Let them shout for joy, and be glad, that favour my righteous cause: yea, let them say continually, "Let the LORD be magnified, which hath pleasure in the prosperity of his servant.'

God takes delight in your fruitfulness.
It gives God the utmost pleasure to see you prosper and succeed in your endeavours. I can imagine God happy and excited when you work things out in your life successfully. And I can see God consulting with the angels and seeking out ways to help you, when you get into a tangle of confusion and despair.

The Bible says in Jeremiah 29:11,
"For I know the thoughts that I think toward you," says the LORD, "thoughts of peace, and not of evil, to give you an expected end."

In III John from verse 2, the Bible says,

Beloved, I wish above all things that thou mayest prosper and be in health, even as thy soul prospereth. For I rejoiced greatly, when the brethren came and

> *testified of the truth that is in thee, even as thou walkest in the truth.*

Friend, your life is destined to be an evidence of the truth, even as you walk in an understanding of this truth. What is the truth? The Lord Jesus Christ is the truth. The Lord Jesus Christ, I believe, in His earthly ministry was most fruitful. Because 2000 years later, His fruits still abide. The truth is that God desires that you be fruitful in your life and that your walk and endeavours abide as Christ's, because the scripture says,

> *"... As my father has sent me, even so send I you."*

It of utmost importance that you understand how Jesus was sent as our redeemer to die in our place, how His life is given to us as an example of the new and living way into God-like fruitfulness.

In Hebrews 10:19-20
> *Having therefore, brethren, boldness to enter into the holiest by the blood of Jesus, By a new and living way, which he hath consecrated for us, through the veil, that is to say, His flesh;*

There is a way now opened up for you and I, into the same land of fruitfulness and impact that was found in our Lord Jesus Christ. He prepared the living way for us by consecrating His flesh. We can also only walk in that way with consecrated flesh and a sanctified mind.

God is the unchanging moulder of destinies, who delights to make Abraham out of Abram's and Israel out of Jacobs.

Wherever you are now there is something higher, more rewarding and more fulfilling ahead of you as you encounter God.

Abraham was nobody, yet he became the father of faith. Jacob was a despised fugitive who became a prince having power to prevail with God and man.

I pray that this book will provoke a life changing encounter in your life in the mighty name of Jesus Christ. It is time to go forward. New horizons beckon to you. The Holy Spirit is willing to guide your feet unto higher grounds. There is always a rock higher than you. It is time to seek higher heights. You will not miss your place of destiny in Jesus' mighty name.

The seed of fruitfulness is planted in you in the person of Jesus Christ at salvation. It's time to take your place and be fruitful. You will not frustrate this grace of God in Jesus' name. There are things to do to guarantee fruitfulness and this is what this book is all about.

In Proverbs 4:7, the Bible says

"Wisdom is the principal thing; therefore get wisdom: with all thy getting get understanding."

Wisdom and understanding are the timeless keys to a life of impact and fruitfulness. They are products of the seed of God's word. When you maximise that seed with determination to bring forth fruit, you provoke divine wisdom, an understanding heart and a destiny of honour, where your function as the light of the world and the salt of the earth becomes established.

KEYS TO FRUITFUL LIFE

CHAPTER ONE

FOUNDATION FOR FRUITFULNESS

In Revelation 3:18, the Bible says,
"I counsel thee to buy of me gold tried in the fire, that thou mayest be rich; and white raiment, that thou mayest be clothed, and that the shame of thy nakedness do not appear; and anoint thine eyes with eyesalve, that thou mayest see."

THE LORD spoke to the last days' church of the need for counsel in prosperity, holiness and revelation knowledge because these are the three keys to fruitfulness and productivity in life. A life that must make impact for God must have and be as the following:

1. Gold tried in fire – This alludes to covenant prosperity; the type that adds no sorrow to it.

2. White raiment – Which is the robe of righteousness that Jesus purchased for us. The only garment that can clothe us before the gates of the thrice holy God.
3. The anointed eye – The object of most of Apostle Paul's prayer in his epistle to the church. It connotes revelation knowledge, insight and understanding.

As you study this book, I see the Lord establish your fruitfulness by confirming these three things in your life.

THE MYSTERY OF THE SEED

The seed of God's word is what grows in our lives to yield the fruits of prosperity, holiness and revelation knowledge. We must understand the mystery of the seed in order to maximise its yield.

The word of God has certain procedural sequences that lead to fulfilment or manifestation of what it promises. God's principles for instance states that only through seed can fruit come; furthermore a seed produces after its kind in multiple folds. In Hebrew the seed is a word called "Zera". This is essentially the element that transmits life. It is the germ cell that contains posterity within it. The seed contains life.

When Jesus said "The words I speak to you are spirit and life", He was saying in essence that, "My words contain seeds that will reproduce my kind of spirit and my kind of life in you."

This is substantiated by Psalm 82:5-7 - God's words therefore have the power to make gods out of us. You can never determine the fruitfulness of a seed by its size neither can the potential of a seed be determined by its external features. Every seed must, however, go through a process to fulfil its ultimate purpose of producing fruits. The more precious the seed, generally, the longer it is processed in the ground. This is true for the seed of God's word also.

The longer you meditate on the word and absorb it to the point of understanding, the more impact it produces in your life.

At creation, there was a divine order in the establishment of the laws that govern nature.

In Genesis 1:11-12,
And God said, Let the earth bring forth grass, the herb yielding seed, and the fruit tree yielding fruit after his kind, whose seed is in itself, upon the earth: and it was so. And the earth brought forth grass, and herb yielding seed after his kind, and the tree yielding fruit, whose seed was in itself, after his kind: and God saw that it was good.

This law of seed propagation came into being before the Law of Fruitfulness. It was later in Genesis 1:28 that we read

> 'And God blessed them, and God said unto them,
> "Be fruitful, and multiply, and replenish the earth,
> and subdue it: and have dominion over the fish of the
> sea, and over the fowl of the air, and over every living
> thing that moveth upon the earth."

The seed is a mystery. The devil understands this mystery and does his worst to ensure people waste their seed or eat up their seed. In every way his purpose is to destroy the seed in order to hinder fruitfulness. God's eternal covenant of fruitfulness is found in Genesis 8:22,

> "While the earth remaineth, seedtime and harvest, cold and heat, summer and winter, and day and night shall not cease."

This is the perpetual covenant between God and man for all generations. There are three things man must do with this covenant:

First, we must hear - Hearing is a process of absorbing and accepting information. Then the second thing to do is to learn - which is the process of understanding the meaning and applications of the information received. While the third is keeping - which is the putting into action the things understood.

This is expressed in Deuteronomy 5:1

And Moses called all Israel and said unto them, "Hear, O Israel, the statues and judgements which I speak in your ears this day that ye may learn them and keep, and do them."

THE MYSTERY OF THE GROUND

Just as the seed is a mystery, the ground is a mystery too. The ground on which the seed is planted determines its maximum yield. Remember the parable of the Lord Jesus in Luke 8:11-15. The ground could represent the nature or character of the recipient of the seed of God's word. In Isaiah 51:1-3 the Bible says,

> *Hearken to me, ye that follow after righteousness, ye that seek the LORD: look unto the rock whence ye are hewn, and to the hole of the pit whence ye are digged. Look unto Abraham your father, and unto Sarah that bare you: for I called him alone, and blessed him, and increased him. For the LORD shall comfort Zion: he will comfort all her waste places; and he will make her wilderness like Eden, and her desert like the garden of the LORD; joy and gladness shall be found therein, thanksgiving, and the voice of melody.*

You don't determine your ground. You only discover your ground. Your ground offers you what is in it. Until you discover what is in your ground and cultivate it, you have no access to liberty. When God planted Eden and positioned Adam in it, Adam did not determine the ground where he was planted. He only discovered it and received his assignment on it. He was to keep the ground in line with God's will. The self will of man was given by God for man to present it back to God, weeded of contrary thoughts and desires.

The same way that no one will plant on an uncultivated field and expect a maximum harvest, God wants us to cultivate and renew our minds. God expects man to constantly express his need for God's nature and to prepare, till and keep their ground in a climate that will enhance the growth of God' nature. God's will is for your life and mine to be as the Garden of the Lord, and our days as heaven on earth.

We are to experience the quintessence of fruitfulness because when God plants a garden it must be fruitful.
God desires to cultivate your Ground.

Fruitfulness is always a witness of God's presence.

In Acts 14:17, the Bible says
"Nevertheless, He left not himself without witness, in that he did good, and gave us rain from heaven, and fruitful seasons, filling our hearts with food and gladness."

Our foundation for fruitfulness is looking at our ground because your life begins to manifest in accordance with your ground. There are certain things about Abraham that established him as the father of faith. If we can discover the treasures of the rock from which we are 'hewn' and the hole of the pit from which we are 'digged' then our fruitfulness will be guaranteed.

Let us take a closer look at Abraham. He had a nature that enhanced the harvest of God's nature; righteousness. He kept his ground in line with God's will. He staggered not. He was strong in faith. He was fully persuaded. He kept giving glory to God.

In Romans 4:20-22 Abraham was described as follows:

He staggered not at the promise of God through unbelief; but was strong in faith, giving glory to God; And being fully persuaded that, what he had promised, he was able also to perform. And therefore it was imputed to him for righteousness.

God's desire is to make your life comfortable, to make your wilderness like Eden and your desert like the garden of the Lord. God wants your life to be full of gladness, thanksgiving and melody, which are signs of success, satisfaction and fulfilment. However, His demand is that you must follow after righteousness.

Unfruitfulness is a curse that must give way in your life forever. Praise God!!! We are no more under a curse when we give our lives to Jesus Christ because Jesus became our spiritual manure. He died and spent three days in the grave and the ground that was cursed became blessed. Jesus who brought life to us also brought fruitfulness. In Him friend, you are planted on the most fruitful hill.

Isaiah 5:1, 2 expresses this
Now will I sing to my well-beloved a song of my beloved touching his vineyard; My well- beloved hath a vineyard in a very fruitful hill: And he fenced it, and gathered out the stones thereof, and planted it with the choicest vine, and built a tower in the midst of it, and also made a winepress therein: and he looked that it should bring forth grapes, and it brought forth wild grapes.

Your life will never bring forth wild grapes unto God in Jesus name; no, wild grapes are not God's expectation for you. From Galatians 3:13, 14, you will discover that one of the benefits of salvation is that you are redeemed from the curse of the law - the curse of poverty, the curse of unfruitfulness - in order to partake of the blessings of Abraham, which he obtained because his stand in faith was imputed to him as righteousness.

Righteousness is uprightness; moral or legal standing, to be just or innocent. This word Righteousness in Hebrew is "Tsedeq". It is used figuratively also to describe prosperity. Amazing!! Simply amazing!! God is saying if you will follow after righteousness you cannot escape fruitfulness and prosperity. It is evident that the foundation of God for fruitfulness and productivity is Holiness and Right Standing.

FOUNDATION OF FRUITFULNESS

This is shown in II Timothy 2:19, 20

Nevertheless the foundation of God standeth sure, having this seal, The Lord knoweth them that are his. And, let every one that nameth the name of Christ depart from iniquity. But in a great house there are not only vessels of gold and of silver, but also of wood and of earth; and some to honour, and some to dishonour.

I pray that you will be a vessel of honour unto God. Can you imagine a stark naked man working on a farm? An uncomfortable thought I am sure. When Adam and Eve were deceived from the way, they became naked fugitives in hiding on the ground that was created for them. A man in hiding is hardly suitable to bring in the harvest. When you are properly dressed in righteousness on your ground, it will bring forth fruit of itself and give you a divine harvest.

Remember what our Lord Jesus Christ said in Mark 4:26-29

And he said, So is the kingdom of God, as if a man should cast seed into the ground; And should sleep, and rise night and day, and the seed should spring and grow up, he knoweth not how. For the earth bringeth forth fruit of herself; first the blade, then the ear, after that the full corn in the ear. But when the fruit is brought forth, immediately he putteth in the sickle, because the harvest is come.

You must be properly clothed before you can dig out the treasures of your ground. When sin struck its deadly blow in Eden, Adam and Even were driven out of comfort into hardship. Genesis 3:24. We also discover from Zechariah 3: 1-7 that when you are not well clothed then you are not well positioned in your ground. You cannot be free to exploit avenues of fruitfulness available to you.

The clothing of the high priest determined his level of freedom, because it was describes as filthy, the enemy could accuse him and stand against him. The first thing God did was to take away the filthy garments on him.

You can only start the journey into fruitfulness when you are properly clothed. In Job 29:14 he said that

"I put on righteousness, and it clothed me: my judgement was as a robe and a diadem."

I want you to pray with me
*"Lord, give me grace to walk with you in righteousness.
Cleanse me by your blood.
Restore my vision and identity.
Give me an insatiable appetite for your presence."*

FOUNDATION OF FRUITFULNESS

KEYS TO FRUITFUL LIFE

CHAPTER TWO

CHARACTERISTICS OF FRUITFULNESS

NOTHING DIES in the realm of the spirit, which is the realm from where our fruitfulness is initiated. God is so interested in your fruitfulness that He made known His established will in Psalm 92:10-15. You can be fruitful even in old age. God's will has no age barriers. Nobody is too old to be fruitful. It is never late with God. Friend, you are never to limit yourself. Jesus already destroyed the works of the devil.

The curse against your fruitfulness is broken. In I John 3:8, the Bible says
"He that committeth sin is of the devil; for the devil sinneth from the beginning. For this purpose the Son of

God was manifested, that he might destroy the works of the devil."

Because of this, you can bring forth fruits right where you are now, even in your old age. He said
"But my horn shalt thou exalt like the horn of an unicorn: I shall be anointed with fresh oil. Mine eye also shall see my desire on mine enemies, and mine ears shall hear my desire of the wicked that rise up against me. The righteous shall flourish like the palm tree: he shall grow like a cedar in Lebanon.
Those that be planted in the house of the LORD shall flourish in the courts of our God. They shall still bring forth fruit in old age; they shall be fat and flourishing; To shew that the LORD is upright: he is my rock, and there is no unrighteousness in him."

READINESS TO HEAR AND OBEY GOD

We have established that the seed of fruitfulness is the Word of God and that life comes from a seed and the life in a seed determines its type of fruit. Therefore on this premise, we can say that no one can be fruitful beyond his level of obedience to the Word of God.

Only quality obedience to God's word will produce quality harvest from God.

CHARACTERISTICS OF FRUITFULNESS

When God gave Jesus Christ to us, He gave Christ to us as a seed and the life in that seed is expected to bring forth fruits in our lives. But our investment of obedience and service to that seed of Christ in us, determines our ultimate fruitfulness in life.

Abraham was a man who kept his ears close to the mouth of God. He was always ready to receive instructions. He was very serious with God. The first thing he did when he arrived at any location was to build an altar of worship and communion with God. Abraham had a listening heart.

He was always ready to obey God. Abraham's faith and obedience as exemplified by his willingness to offer Isaac did not start in Genesis 22.

It started way back in Genesis 12 when we first met Abraham when he departed from his family and kindred. It was also demonstrated as he gave up Hagar and Ishmael.

In Genesis 17:23 the quality of Abraham's devotion and obedience to God's word is portrayed as he circumcised both himself and every male under his jurisdiction on the same day that God commanded him.

It is this degree of obedience to the word of life that we must embrace to enjoy fruitfulness.

We need to follow this intense worship and devotion to God to enjoy His best. It takes a relationship with God where our ears are close to His mouth to enjoy the benefits of His leading.

MEEKNESS

Abraham was also an extremely meek man. In Genesis 13, his nephew Lot, had followed him into Egypt and when Abraham came out of Egypt he was so blessed that Lot by virtue of association was blessed too. However, a misunderstanding came up between the herdsmen of Abraham and Lot. And through this simple event we catch a glimpse of the quality and integrity of the character of Abraham. Under normal circumstances you would have expected Abraham, as the uncle, to have first choice of which direction he wanted to go. But in Genesis 13:10, 11 the Bible says

10And Lot lifted up his eyes, and beheld all the plain of Jordan, that it was well watered every where, before the LORD destroyed Sodom and Gomorrah, even as the garden of the LORD, like the land of Egypt, as thou comest unto Zoar.   11Then Lot chose him all the plain of Jordan; and Lot journeyed east: and they separated themselves the one from the other

It later took the intercession and intervention of Abraham to deliver Lot and his family from this carnal choice. On the other hand it was God who helped Abraham to choose.

CHARACTERISTICS OF FRUITFULNESS

God lifted up the eyes of Abraham and showed him his inheritance. In the Sermon on the Mount Jesus said, *"Blessed are the meek, for they shall inherit the earth."*

In Psalm 25:9, the Bible also says
"The meek will he guide in judgement and the meek will he teach his ways."

It is evident therefore that meekness is a principal quality of the soul that enables us to receive instruction from God's word which in turn leads to fruitfulness. The seed of fruitfulness is the Word of God.

In James 1:18, the Bible says
"Of his own will begat he us with the word of truth, that we should be kind of first fruits of his creature."

God is the father of light and the
"entrance of His word gives light."

The seed that brings this order of fruitfulness in which every good and perfect inheritance is given to us is His word. If the world came into being by His word according to Hebrews 11:3 then your world and your life can also blossom and come into fruitfulness by His word. Genuine fruitfulness in life begins with the implantation of the seed of the Word of God. Luke 8:11, the Bible says, "the seed is the word of God." In Luke 1:38, Mary said, "Let it be unto me according to thy word."

There is no genuine scriptural fruitfulness outside the word of God. Jesus Christ is called The Sun of righteousness.

In Malachi 4:2, the Bible says
"But unto you that fear my name shall the Sun of righteousness arise with healing in his wings; and ye shall go forth, and grow up as calves of the stall."

In the natural, on our planet earth, it is the sun that provides the energy for life. Without the sun we cannot be talking about life on earth. The same way, Jesus Christ is the Sun of Righteousness that guarantees fruitfulness and productivity.

In the spiritual, He is the one that provides the spiritual energy for godly living. The Bible calls us

"Trees of Righteousness, the Planting of the Lord"
Isaiah 61:3.

Therefore our position relative to the rays of the sun of righteousness (influences of His Spirit) and how deep our roots are in the waters of His word determines how juicy the fruit of our lives will be. I pray that this Sun of righteousness will shine in all His radiance on you and bring healing to you, bring deliverance and joy. I pray that you will go forth, progress, grow up, and be productive. You will tread down the wicked and you will prosper in Jesus Christ's precious name. Amen.

CHARACTERISTICS OF FRUITFULNESS

PHYSICAL CONDITIONS FOR WORD PRODUCTIVITY

Let us quickly examine what I call physical requirements for the success of the word of God in our lives. I believe these were conditions fulfilled in the life of Abraham that made him great. As we analyse this thing together greatness is on your way in Jesus' name. Amen.

In the natural when a farmer takes a seed the first thing he looks at closely is the environment in which the seed is to be planted. He will want to examine the soil texture and the climate in which he will plant that seed which is of great value to him. Similarly as far as God is concerned His words to us are exceedingly great and precious. Nobody throws precious seeds carelessly anywhere. If God promises are precious to Him, they ought to be more precious to us.

II Peter 1:4 tells us, *"His words are precious promises."* In the physical, the earth or soil represents the place where the seed is sacrificed because when you plant a seed, it is like a sacrifice. You actually don't know what goes on underneath the earth. Planting is always an act of faith. The seed may or may not come up. However, in the spiritual the seed which is the word of God, is incorruptible. It cannot be faulted. In I Peter 1:23, the Bible says,

> *"Being born again, not of corruptible seed, but of incorruptible, by the word of God, which liveth and abideth forever."*

The heart of man is the soil in which this incorruptible seed is planted. The quality of the heart invariably determines the quality of fruitfulness. Remember the parable of the sower in Matthew 13:8 and 23. Our hearts represents the field in which God decides to sacrifice precious and exceedingly great seeds. That same parable in Luke 8:15 says,

> *"But that on the good ground are they, which in an honest and good heart, having heard the word, keep it, and bring forth fruit with patience."*

The good ground with the highest yield of fruitfulness is the honest and understanding heart. It takes understanding to be fruitful. We need to ask God for understanding.

Understanding is not just hearing but hearing to the point of productive application in practical and immediate issues of our lives.

An honest heart is a heart devoid of pretence and free from self-deceit. It is conscientious and truthful. It takes an honest and understanding heart for the word of God to be fruitful in your life. Many people come to church and all they want is a beautiful sermon and excitement.

But ask them one hour later what the message was, they will not remember although they may have shouted the loudest Amen during that service.

This is what Apostle James aptly described in James 1:22-25,
²²But be ye doers of the word, and not hearers only, deceiving your own selves. ²³For if any be a hearer of the word, and not a doer, he is like unto a man beholding his natural face in a glass: ²⁴For he beholdeth himself, and goeth his way, and straightway forgetteth what manner of man he was. ²⁵But whoso looketh into the perfect law of liberty, and continueth therein, he being not a forgetful hearer, but a doer of the work, this man shall be blessed in his deed.

Those he describes as hearers only, never mix the word with faith and understanding because they do not apply the principle of heart preparation.

HEART PREPARATION FOR FRUITFULNESS

When you locate a piece of ground you don't just throw your seed all over the place. There must be some degree of preparation. Something needs to be done in our hearts before we present it to the Lord for him to sow his exceeding great and precious seeds. When we do the proper thing, honesty and understanding will be integrated in our hearts to bring fruitfulness. Let's examine this parable in Luke 13:6-9,

> ^{6}He spake also this parable; A certain man had a fig tree planted in his vineyard; and he came and sought fruit thereon, and found none. ^{7}Then said he unto the dresser of his vineyard, Behold, these three years I come seeking fruit on this fig tree, and find none: cut it down; why cumbereth it the ground? ^{8}And he answering said unto him, Lord, let it alone this year also, till I shall dig about it, and dung it: ^{9}And if it bear fruit, well: and if not, then after that thou shalt cut it down.

This is a parable where we see our Lord Jesus Christ advocating for us as the dresser of the vineyard and in Verse 8, we see His treatment or his remedy for preparing a heart or ground. God demands fruitfulness and progress so that he can take delight in our prosperity.

What hinders many people from bearing fruit is that they come into the presence of God with unprepared hearts. Many people's hearts are unkempt. If you should have ability to see the nature of the hearts people bring into God's presence for implantation of His seed you will see for instance many gorgeously dressed people on Sunday morning whose hearts within are so filthy that they look like someone who has not had a bath in 3 weeks. The heart could be stinking, dirty, unprepared, uncultivated. It could be hardened, sceptical, and full of excuses. It's like trying to plant a seed of corn on a cement floor. However, Jesus talks of digging about it. What does this mean? Digging our hearts in preparation refers to repentance. In Acts 2:38

CHARACTERISTICS OF FRUITFULNESS

"Then Peter said unto them, Repent, and be baptised every one of you in the name of Jesus Christ for the remission of sins, and ye shall receive the gift of the Holy Ghost."

There is no receptivity until there is repentance. We need to approach God with a heart of repentance. For instance we need to pray to God:

Father, I know I should know more about You than I do now. Lord, forgive me. I desire to know You because I need You. My soul thirsts for You. Without You Lord I can do nothing. Lord, forgive my carelessness in the past in my relationship with You. Forgive me for those days I just sleep and I do nothing. Forgive me for neglecting Your word. Forgive me for ignoring the Holy Spirit. Lord, forgive me. As I come today, give me understanding. Draw me to yourself. Lord, receive me as I receive Your word.

This is the process of digging up your heart, breaking the fallow ground, turning over the soil so you can present fresh and turned-over soil to God.

Furthermore Jesus said "And dung it". To dung means to fertilise it or enrich it or nourish it, to guarantee the fruitfulness of the incorruptible seed. How do we fertilise our hearts? We fertilise our hearts through prayer.

As you commune with God in prayer and intercede for the church service you are about to attend and you pray for the pastor, the dew of heaven begins to descend on your heart and your heart becomes moist and ready for the word of God. In the physical we know that wise farmers always plant when the soil is moist because there is a better guarantee of germination.

Many Christians come to church and think they are doing the pastor a favour; some even come before God and they have no purpose. They think, "well it's a religious duty" and they just come. They have no expectation and so there is no manifestation. The presence of God is the place where you receive the seed of fruitfulness. Therefore before you come into the presence of God you owe yourself a duty to go on your knees and commune with Him.

Father, I come forth to receive your exceeding great and precious promises. Because they are precious to you Lord, they are doubly precious to me. You have said "So shall your word be that proceeds from Your mouth, it shall not go unfulfilled." Lord, make my heart a prepared place. Your word cannot fail in my life. Every deception is cast out of my heart in the name of Jesus Christ. Lord, give me this day a word for me. Give me a word that will transform my life. Your word is powerful. Lord, grant me access into divine insight that will lead me into fruitfulness and fulfilment.

This is the way to prepare our hearts. This is the way to approach God's word. Lack of preparation is mainly the reason why many people are not fulfilled. We are too careless concerning the things of God. Imagine for instance, if the president of your country should give you an appointment in which he grants you fifteen minutes to present a certain issue to him. I can assure you that you will prepare.

Many will not sleep all night, rehearsing their presentation. They will gather facts; collate figures so they can appear authentic. This is the same attitude we need to have as we approach God for any kind of service. God looks at the heart and instead of being authentic many are fake and full of misconceptions, assumptions and self deceit. You should talk to God and prepare for your meeting with Him. Don't presume. Dig up your heart and dung it. Planting your seed when the ground is moist is the sound advice for farmers; the same goes for Christians.

Take your heart into the presence of God, moist and ready, wet with the dew of heaven, the Holy Ghost already brooding over your heart, then you will see the creative forces of God manifesting in your life.

See what God did in the life of this brother as a result of his prepared heart, "I was terribly indebted when I became a born-again Christian two months ago. I can't explain how these debts have been mysteriously paid off except by the power of God's word, which I have been receiving in church. The truth really liberates.

My business also took a new turn upwards after I boldly ministered the word of God and gave a potential senior business partner a copy of the church's publication.

Contrary to the lie of Satan that it will put her off; she was excited and gave me better terms than I bargained for."

SPIRITUAL CONDITIONS FOR WORD PRODUCTIVITY

Now, we must also appraise what happens to the seed when it enters the ground. When the physical conditions are met when the seed is sown certain things also happen in the unseen realm. In the natural when the seed enters the ground the process of germination begins and the plumule and radicle begin to express themselves. Spiritually, just like a natural seed, first decays in order to empower the new life that shoots out as the stem and the root, the same way we must die to self before we can arise in the newness and power of the life from the word of God.

In John 12:24 the Bible says,
"Verily, verily, I say unto you, Except a corn of wheat fall to ground and die, it abideth alone: but if it die, it bringeth forth much fruit."

Before the Word of God can yield maximally in our lives we must die to sense knowledge and our opinions. In the tabernacle of Moses the first thing you encounter as you enter the door is the Altar of Sacrifice; in Exodus 27. This is the place of sacrifice where God gave up His best for us. This is where blood is shed. This is where we are

CHARACTERISTICS OF FRUITFULNESS

required also to give up our best for God. His thoughts are higher than our thoughts and His ways higher than our ways. Until we take the word of God hook, line and sinker and nothing else matters but God and His word we cannot be truly fruitful. Jesus Christ never questioned or reasoned away the will of God, He offered himself as a perfect sacrifice. The same way God expects us to present ourselves a living sacrifice and to embrace His ways as we die to ours.

This is the place where Abraham gave up Isaac. This is where we are also expected to give up our Isaac. The Bible instructs in Romans 12:1- 2

¹I beseech you therefore, brethren, by the mercies of God, that ye present your bodies a living sacrifice, holy, acceptable unto God, which is your reasonable service. ²And be not conformed to this world: but be ye transformed by the renewing of your mind, that ye may prove what is that good, and acceptable, and perfect, will of God.

The truth is this; there is nothing God can do on earth without man because God already gave man dominion. In Psalm 8:6, He says,
"Thou madest him to have dominion over the works of thy hands; thou hast put all things under his feet."

When Jesus came and redeemed us, He corrected the error of Adam and gave back to everyone who believes in Him the power to reign in dominion. In Psalm 103:7 we discover that Moses understood the ways of God – that is the way of total submission and death to self – while the children of Israel only saw the acts or the manifestation of the ways of God. God could not deliver Israel without Moses. Throughout the Bible in the relationship of God and men, God always needed a man to deliver other men. But until a man is dead to self he cannot be fruitful for God's purpose.

So how do we begin to die to self? We begin by waiting on the Lord; seeking His face in study and prayer. Waiting on the Lord, I believe, is not necessarily fasting but may include fasting; however it is an intense undisrupted fellowship with God. As we spend time with God something of God rubs off on us. We begin to die to self – to our carnal reasoning and fleshy lust; and we start to grow keen in the awareness of the mind and thoughts of God.

We die to self in fellowship with God exposing our flesh to the radiance of His majesty through prayer, study of His word and fasting from food to subdue our flesh and appetite.

Truly, as we begin to spend qualitative time with God we begin to shoot down our roots into great waters and bear fruit in our seasons just as the word of God says in

Psalm 1:1-3
1Blessed is the man that walketh not in the counsel of the ungodly, nor standeth in the way of sinners, nor sitteth in the seat of the scornful. 2But his delight is in

CHARACTERISTICS OF FRUITFULNESS

the law of the LORD; and in his law doth he meditate day and night. ³And he shall be like a tree planted by the rivers of water, that bringeth forth his fruit in his season; his leaf also shall not wither; and whatsoever he doeth shall prosper.

New life must be a submitted life. What happens next? When a seed dies, new life is produced. The new life is always after the kind of the seed that was planted in the first place. When you begin to die to self and receive the incorruptible word of grace, a new life is produced in you after the order of Jesus Christ. Christ – life or an anointed life bearing the presence of God begins to be produced in you and that is when the Bible says

"We all come in the unity of the faith, and of the knowledge of the Son of God, until perfect man, until the measure of the stature of the fullness of Christ."
(Ephesians 4:13)

Jesus, I believe, is a type of the Tree of Life. He is eternally bearing fruit because He died to self. He gave up His will to the will of the father and today eternally, He still bears fruit. So it takes dying to self, taking the word of God as the gospel truth, despising symptoms and circumstances, receiving and believing prophetic declarations from the word of God to bear fruits. When we receive and stand on the word of God we have a guarantee of fruitfulness. Sometimes the world may mock at you or make a fool of you but Jesus said, "Wisdom is justified of her children". The wisdom of God, in His word you put your trust in, will always justify you.

It is time for us to be married to Him who was raised from the dead in order to bring forth fruits unto God. We need this new life that comes as a result of dying to self. It should be a desire in our hearts. No one can teach another person how to die except He that died and rose again; Jesus Christ. It is to Him we must go. "Unto Shiloh we must come." God is tired of denominationalism and our smug Pentecostalism. God is calling us into something more intimate than the baptism of the Holy Spirit and speaking in tongues. God is demanding a deeper fellowship with us that require dying to self, dying to the senses and its fleshy lust and standing on the truth of God in absolute trust. This is what it takes to be connected to the eternal fountain of fruitfulness. Hallelujah!!

Jesus said in John 15:7,
"If ye abide in me, and my words abide in you, ye shall ask what ye will, and it shall be done unto you."

So what does it mean to abide? It means to obey unquestionably, to dwell in, and to accept on a lasting or permanent basis. When we truly understand what it means to abide, prayer will not be a struggle. Fellowship in the word will not be a wrestle. People who are abiding know that, it is the source of their existence.

They fellowship with God until the fellowship with God is like the very blood flowing in their veins and the very air they breathe. When they miss fellowship they feel like they are choking. Until fellowship with God becomes as valuable as life itself you may not bring forth the maximum harvest from the seed of God's word implanted in you.

Although it is true that the grace of God and his tender mercies are new everyday, for any serious Christian who desires to be engaged by God in these end time, you need to do something more. There must be a greater desire in your heart to do something for God – to abide in fellowship with God, to have a right relationship with God. Don't pray to have God. Pray that God may have you. But note that God will not have you except you are dead to self. God had to take Moses through 40 years of tempering His Spirit and teaching him how to herd a flock of sheep. At the end the Bible said

"Moses was the meekest of all men on the face of the earth"
(Num 12:3).

It was God who taught him. He had not always been like that because in Acts7:22, he was said to be mighty in word and deed. But he had to shed the learning of Egypt to embrace and abide in the everlasting truth of God's wisdom. Before God's word can truly become fruitful and for God to use us as instruments for His glory we must submit to God. We must die to self and learn to abide in Him and live in His word. It must become our meditation day and night. That is the only way to be truly fruitful.

Let us carefully consider that there is something more beyond abiding. A woman can be married and abide in her husband's house but she may not yield to him. It is not enough to abide in the word. We must yield our will absolutely to the dictates of the word.

There are some people that are a walking concordance. They can quote the entire Bible. They have memorised it. But it does not reflect in their lives. They spend time to memorise the word but sometimes it is only for a display; they are not yielding to the Spirit and the demands of the word. These people become instructors who themselves have not been instructed in God. When a situation occurs they would have reacted in the flesh before coming back to the word because though it seems they are abiding in the word, the word is not abiding in them. When the word truly begins to abide in us, it comes to the forefront always in our dealings with the issues of life. What the Holy Scriptures say becomes a response of our being to circumstances as the word of God and the Holy Spirit begin to guide and rule every aspect of our lives. We are given the word as the vehicle for partaking of God's divine nature.

In II Peter 1:3, 5
^{3}According as his divine power hath given unto us all things that pertain unto life and godliness, through the knowledge of him that hath called us to glory and virtue: ^{5}And beside this, giving all diligence, add to your faith virtue; and to virtue knowledge;"

We must give all diligence to add to our faith in the word virtue; that is honour, principle, uprightness, morality.

CHARACTERISTICS OF FRUITFULNESS

We must walk diligently to demonstrate the virtue in the word. We need to make serious efforts as Christians and ask for the wisdom of God that will enable us to practically apply the truth in God's word in our lives. Jesus was a hard worker. He was diligent. In John 4:1-34 at the well of Jacob, Jesus was so tired physically; He was also hungry. He was so thirsty that all His disciples went to fetch food for Him to be refreshed. But immediately He saw an opportunity to minister, his strength was revived.

That should be our nature. We must be revived and happy to work with and for God. Wisdom says in Hebrews 6:12, *"That ye be not slothful, but followers of them who through faith and patience inherit the promises."*

We should follow those who have obtained.

Jesus was an epitome of diligence.

He preached all day and always rose up a great while before dawn to pray and fellowship with the Father because He was sustained in His ministry by the Holy Spirit.

Remember in Luke 4:14 "Jesus returned in the power of the Spirit." The Spirit is simply the breath of God. In the day Jesus performed miracles. Long before dawn through the night He stays in the presence of God for God's breath of new freshness and unction.
Thus He contacts the inspiration of the Almighty.

Remember Job 32:8. When you arrive at God's presence, His presence and His breath envelopes you and inspire your heart or gives light to your spirit and you receive the power and the unction to do things for God. You cannot afford to be idle because idleness is a curse and laziness is a trap of hell.

In Ecclesiastes 10:18, the Bible says,
"By much slothfulness the building decays; and through idleness of the hands the house drops through."

There is great joy in cultivating the presence of God because God is the author of fruitfulness.

When you cultivate God's presence in His word and in prayer you cannot help but be fruitful.

There is a journey from our mind to our heart which we must make. There is the Son of God, the teachings and there is the life of the Son of God. Very often we end up only knowing the Son but not the life of the Son. We recognise the Son in our mind but the life of the son can only be lived from our hearts.

It is time to make lasting decisions about your life my friend. You can decide right now whether you want to remain the same. As for me I do not ever want God to find me in the same spiritual state year after year. I am ready. I am hungry for more of God.

CHARACTERISTICS OF FRUITFULNESS

Lord, draw me closer to you. I receive more grace to run after you. Let my desire be you. Let my focus and my entire being be centred on you. Make me run after you my Father. Draw me by your spirit. Enable me Lord, to pursue you as my primary love and to live daily with you in sweet fellowship.

I pray that right now you will sincerely open your mouth and express your hunger to God. Ask Him to give you an insatiable appetite for his presence. Ask him to draw you closer. Ask to be clothed in his glory and majesty and your destiny of fruitfulness shall be guaranteed.

KEYS TO FRUITFUL LIFE

CHAPTER THREE

RELEASING GOD'S SEED OF FRUITFULNESS IN YOU

THE SEED of glory, fruitfulness and abundance is planted within us when we give our lives to Jesus Christ. It is our salvation that connects us to a most fruitful vine. However, we must release and harness the potential of that seed as shown in John 15:1-7

¹I am the true vine, and my Father is the husbandman. ²Every branch in me that beareth not fruit he taketh away: and every branch that beareth fruit, he purgeth it, that it may bring forth more fruit. ³Now ye are clean through the word which I have spoken unto you. ⁴Abide in me, and I in you. As the branch cannot bear fruit of itself, except it abide in the vine; no more can ye, except ye abide in me. ⁵I am the vine, ye are the branches: He that abideth in me, and I in him, the same bringeth forth much fruit: for without me ye can do nothing. ⁶If a man abide not in me, he is cast forth as a branch, and is withered; and men gather them, and cast them into the fire, and they are burned. ⁷If ye abide in me, and my words abide in you, ye shall ask what ye will, and it shall be done unto you.

There is this practical aspect of fruitfulness, which we shall examine in this third chapter and I see the anointing of God being released into your life already as you continue reading this book in Jesus' mighty name.

The Bible says,
"He that tileth his land shall have plenty of bread: but he that followeth after vain persons shall have poverty enough"
(Proverbs 28:19).

What then is your land? In the scripture, land is a type of life. Just like in every land there is a deposit of certain treasures so it is in every man's life. There is a deposit of treasures.

When a man is connected to Christ through salvation he has access to the rich deposits of God but it takes tilling it or working it, to bring out the treasure.

God put Adam in a garden of plenty in which God himself planted and provided everything. Yet Adam was instructed to till it and keep it. That was Adam's assignment and it is still our assignment today. The gifts of God are without repentance.

Your assignment for your life is to till your life, discover the treasures that God has deposited within you.

It is a walk of responsibility with God as we continue to till our land for we are labourers together with God. That is, we are God's cultivated field. By the time you finish reading this book I pray that God would have provoked the treasures within you to be stirred up. Your life will no more be hidden. Your star will shine out of obscurity in the name of Jesus Christ.

Whosoever is faithful in this assignment of tilling his land shall abide in blessings, according to Proverbs 28:20. This connotes fruitfulness. The assignment of life is to dig out the treasures, the possibilities, the potentials that are available to us.

However, there is a kind of satanic oppression and bondage that holds down a lot of believers. It is the spirit of nonchalance. "Take it easy. When we get to heaven we shall enjoy everything. Let us eat and sleep." This is the spirit of the worthless servant. In Matthew 25:14-30, at least his master thought he was worth one talent but this servant showed himself as totally worthless.

Blessings are a function of what you do with the treasures of God in your life.

Whatever makes you to be nonchalant and careless about the gifts that God has deposited in your life is cursed today in Jesus' name. Don't sit in idleness. Don't lie down in limbo and expect God to come and do everything for you. He has already done what he will do and he's watching over his word to perform it. He has already given his word and given his Spirit. All things are upheld and sustained by that word. If you are waiting for God you may wait for eternity. Start acting on the word now.

We think in time dimension but God is not a God of time. He is I AM; a God of now. Eternity for God is a continuous now. By faith we can break through the timeline mentality and receive all of God now. Free yourself please. Don't get caught in that time trap. Reach out in faith to God. Proverbs 13:23 the Bible says,

"Much food is in the tillage of the poor: but there is that is destroyed for want of judgement."

You cannot be nonchalant about life. Please permit me to interpret Proverbs 13:23 with inferences from other scriptures like in John 6:48-55 Jesus said,

"I am the bread of life." He said, "my flesh is meat indeed, my blood is drink indeed."

Therefore we can interpret Proverbs 13:23 as follows: much of Jesus is in the ground of the poor but He is destroyed for lack of understanding of how to release the Jesus within him.

Success in Christendom is not so much a subject of comparison. It is really how much of Jesus inside you that you can release.

The treasures of success are the deposits of His Holy Spirit within us. How much of him finds expression in us is the true measure of our success.

The day we experience the new birth, each one receives a blank cheque to collect blessings from heaven. God doesn't determine what is written on that cheque, we do. The same cheque leaf that carries $100 can also cash $1,000,000,000. The difference is in the thinking process within the person writing the cheque and how big the kingdom of God is in his or her heart.

When we are born again our spirit is recreated to have fellowship with the Holy Spirit. That is the same Spirit of God who wrote the Bible and who empowered Jesus.

He said,
"Behold I give unto you power to tread upon serpents and scorpion and over all the power of the enemy and nothing shall by any means hurt you." Power to do what? Well He said "power to tread upon serpents and scorpions";

The creeping crawling creatures, the distractions and the deceptions of the devil. The power that overcomes shame is with Jesus. The way upward is inward. This is like a mystery. The way up is not abroad. It is inward. The power to release fruitfulness is already inside you. Apostle Paul said in Philippians 4:13
"I can do all things through Christ which strengtheneth me."

Where does the strength come from? Where does He strengthen us from? It is not from outside. It is from within. Jesus said in John 6:63
"The words that I speak to you, they are spirit and life."

Until that word connects with your spirit man there is no release of strength.

The strength is within. The treasures are within. The gifts of God are within. I look around and I see great potentials in people all around me. There are certain treasures deposited in every life. If you don't till your land, dig it and bring it out you can have all the best from heaven and go to the grave in a full old age without realising the fruits of such potentials.

We are blessed already. Ephesians 1:3
"Blessed be the God and Father of our Lord Jesus Christ, who hath blessed us with all spiritual blessings in heavenly places in Christ."

Why would the Bible put this in past tense? Where is Jesus now? Jesus is in heavenly places seated on the right hand of majesty according to Ephesians 2:6. If we are seated together with Him and He's seated in heavenly places doesn't this appear like a contradiction? No. He living in us and we, abiding in him, is what establishes our position in heavenly places. We are one with Him in the mystery of marriage. He is our head and we are his body. Remember that in Ephesians 5 from verse 23 the Bible says,

23For the husband is the head of the wife, even as Christ is the head of the church: and he is the saviour of the body. 24Therefore as the church is subject unto Christ, so let the wives be to their own husbands in every thing. 25Husbands, love your wives, even as Christ also loved the church, and gave himself for it;

Christ represents us in heaven as our high priests and we represent him here as ambassadors reconciling men and women to Him. He is seated where every resource is available at the fountain of life, the place of unlimited fruitfulness representing us.

Everything God owns is therefore available to us in Christ. But just like diamonds are not picked on the surface we have to dig for it.

There are treasures inside you; they are precious but also available. It is time to reach within and begin to pull them out. We are destined to come to the fullness of the stature of Christ. The battle is not so much to get Christ into us as to release the Christ that is already within us and to allow Him to find practical expression.

This is where we need the help of Holy Spirit. The way God thinks is different from how we think. But God desires that we think like Him. God is always working from the invisible to manifest the visible. The nature of God is that, God keeps seeing that which is yet to be done. He told Abraham in Genesis 13:14
"Lift up now thine eyes, and look from the place where thou art northward, and southward, and eastward, and westward: For all the land which thou seest, to thee will I give it, and to thy seed forever."

God accepted Abraham's faith and counted it as righteousness. The greatest hindrance to our faith sometimes may be that which we can see, our immediate success or that which we have accomplished.

The status you have or who you are, is not so relevant to God. What is relevant to God now is what you can become that you have not yet become.

Immediately you see the world only from the perspective of your achievements, you may lose the possibility of releasing the next thing God has in store for you.

There is much more in God for you than what you are tackling now. Release it in Jesus' name. God always sees

the invisible first. In Hebrews 11:1, the Bible says
"Now faith is the substance of things hoped for, the evidence of things not seen."

Let me assure you: whatever we can see in the physical began its journey from the invisible realm. It started as an idea or a thought and inspiration in someone's mind. Maybe it occurred to several people at the same time. That thought or idea, although tangible, is invisible. It is hope.

Now this is how God operates and how He wants us to operate. When inspired thoughts come into our hearts, a door of hope is knocked upon.

Hope wakes up. However, faith is the evidence of hope; the substance, the activity, the working out of our hope. The idea is the hope.

But until you begin to take steps to work it out, thinking through, praying, sowing the word of God relevant to the idea, what constitutes the substance of your faith that fulfils hope is never released.

Everything we buy with money today came from the invisible realm. Someone invested time and faith until it became a visible and valuable reality that must be paid for. This is God's method.

We have read the story of creation as written by Moses

and we literally imagine God only said "Let there be light" and everything began to fall in place. However, Prophet Isaiah gives us a deeper insight. In Isaiah 48:13, the Bible says,

"Mine hand also hath laid the foundation of the earth, and my right hand hath spanned the heavens: when I call unto them, they stand up together."

God obviously had done some preparatory work. His hand first went to work to spread out the things he wanted to do. He had it well reasoned out before He began to call out the "Let there be". What God called out to be were things He had silently worked out. When I call, it is because I have already done something that will enable them to stand up and be presentable as I call.

Nobody has a monopoly of ideas.

Sometimes when God releases an idea, many people who are receptive will catch it. However, until somebody pleases God by taking steps of faith, God will continue to release the idea to as many people as are receptive to him until His purpose is achieved.

I once watched Evangelist Reinhard Bonnke on video. He spoke about a project God gave him. God had instructed him to print a classic presentation of the gospel of Jesus Christ and put it in the hand of every family on earth. He said when God spoke to him, he pointed out to God how busy he already was how his schedule was so tight and God told him, "You were not my first choice. You are the third. I already spoke to two of my servants but they were so occupied with their own projects they could not receive my own project."

From this, the reality of how it is very easy to miss the programme of God dawned on me.

Many may have missed God a long time ago yet they are pursuing and exercising faith for things of no enduring value.

Once we are born again, our spirit man is opened to catch ideas from God. But if we don't do anything about it, God will bypass us and look for someone else to do something about it. What you need first is not necessarily money.

What you need is a good idea. If you have a good practical idea and the wisdom of how to go about it, money will beg you to execute that project. A lot of people are wasting their lives waiting for capital when all that they need is capital-sense. It is time to dig within and venture without.

It is time for Christians to step out and utilize the gifts of God deposited in us for our benefit and the benefit of mankind. Please don't limit yourself. You cannot fail. Failure is in not trying at all. Be confident. Be bold. The greater one is in you. There is no handicap you cannot overcome.

I remember the testimony of a young man whose office

was in his briefcase. He was a supplier of computer parts. He walked into one of his client's office one morning and the managing director said "look, we are not interested in computer now. I need to get eight cars from Peugeot automobiles Nigeria." Quickly the boy's head did a mental arithmetic and he said "I can supply the cars."

I believe intelligence is the ability to respond positively to possibilities. Many people watch opportunities pass them by everyday and are defeated before they have taken any step. If there was no prompting in the heart of that man he would have lost out that contract, but he got it. Hallelujah!

That man must have reasoned
"Hey Jesus is in me. Even if I don't know this thing, there must be somebody who knows it."

A consultant is merely someone who knows how to effectively consult those who know.

I read of Henry Ford, the car inventor or manufacturer. Some people challenged him to court, labelling him an illiterate. They began to ask him a lot of questions. They said "What is the longest river in the world. What is the distance from the sun to the earth?"

Well, Henry Ford just kept looking at them. After they were pleased that they had made their point he addressed the jury and his accusers and said, "I don't have the time to answer those foolish questions. On my office desk I have a row of buttons. I can press anyone of those buttons and get one of my managers to supply me with any information I need."

I believe intelligence is the ability to get required information when you need it. It is different from education. Many educators, teachers and lecturers are suffering but some people who never went to school who are selling nails or roofing sheets have built mansions and estates. They are more knowledgeable about their local economy and the sub region where they have doors of interaction than the theoretical economists teaching in the classroom.

Many people have a Masters Degree but they are not masters of anything.

Remember the treasures of God are within you. Begin to dig it out. Everything we can see now can be improved upon. It is your ability to dig from within to add to the things you can see that creates wealth and fruitfulness. The seed is within.

We need to understand who we are to know the possibilities available to us. In the spirit realm, who you are is determined by who you are connected to. When you are born again you are connected to God through Jesus by the Holy Spirit. That means all possibilities are opened to you.

Do you know that unbelievers also receive ideas and they make money and are fruitful from such ideas? But some Christians are sitting down and waiting for the day angel Gabriel will appear. Other believers condemn themselves and look down on themselves while many are pushed aside because of their negative self-image. But we are children of God.

Our limitation is not in what people say, neither is it in how we feel.

God does such limits on our lives. If you think you can't make it you never will. Because
"*as a man thinketh so is he.*"

God will never violate your will. It is not an issue of prayer. If you confidently trust in God, God will give you the fuel and the energy for as far as your eyes or imaginations can go.

In Judges 6, we encounter Gideon; a man who did not know himself. That's the trouble with too many believers. We need to trust God that He knows more about us than we know ourselves.

If you can connect with what God is saying about you, you will achieve valiant things like Gideon, later known as a mighty man of valour. Eternal victories are opened to you as you take your place in destiny.

Jacob got to a point in his life where he was caught between the devil and the deep blue sea. Here he was: he had just made a covenant with Laban never to cross back in Syria yet he could not go forward because of the threat of Esau who was approaching with 400 armed men.

> ***Until many people get to this point in life, where they are desperate and can't go forward or backwards, they never look up.***

Jacob got hold of God and he must have said, "Lord I'm disgusted with myself and I refuse to see myself. I even refuse to acknowledge how people see me. How do you see me Lord? What do you have in me? What have you put in me?" Jacob desperately single handedly fought an angel to a stand-still spiritually.

Yet, when the angel asked him "What is your name". He replied, "Jacob" meaning supplanter and cheat. But the angel said "No.

You are mistaken. It's true that name was given as a circumstance of your birth dictated. The name found expression due to pressures around you but that is not god's destiny for you. God does not call you Jacob. God calls you Israel; a prince with God." You need to understand and know what God calls you. Look at the case of Apostle Peter.

"And when Jesus beheld him," John 1:42,
'He said, "Thou art Simon the son of Jona: thou shalt be called Cephas, which is by interpretation, A stone."'

Simon Bar Jonah is such an interesting combination of names. Simon means a reed; a tender water plant easily swayed here and there by water currents and Jonah, off course we must remember, the reluctant prophet Jonah who had to spend 3 days in the belly of the whale before deciding to fulfil his assignment. So literally Peter's name was - instability son of reluctance. Both names connoted an indecisive personality.

But Jesus came and said "No. You can't fulfil your calling with that name. You don't know who you are. You are from the foundation of the earth Peter, a rock." Can you compare a rock and a reed? What a contrast.

We need to connect to our roots and locate destiny. There is a name God is calling you. Won't you like to find out? As you discover it, your destiny will enter the realm of super fruitfulness.

God wants you to have peace. He wants you to have an expected end. There is an expected end in the heart of God. There is a level of fruitfulness and success that God is expecting from you.

There is great hope in the heart of God concerning your future, your productivity and your success and God is saying, "My goodwill is available for you. If you will cooperate with me and make my hope a reality in your life."

You never realise that destiny while merely sitting down.

You only realise it by digging up the deposits of the gifts of God that is in you. Colossians 1:27 says,
"Christ in you the hope of glory."

There is something inside you that God is expecting. Many are reading right now who are multi millionaires waiting to be revealed. Many are intellectuals. Others are industrialists about to harness the seed of fruitfulness that is within them into a mighty harvest.

The riches of God's glory are unquantifiable.

You can't really measure it and the Bible says,
> "That mystery of immeasurable riches of God's glory dwells in us in the person of Christ Jesus."

Please forget about errors in your past. Some destinies are tied down by past mistakes. Don't anchor your life around any error in the past. Proverbs 24:16 says,

> "For a just man falleth seven times, and riseth up again: but the wicked shall fall into mischief."

Rise up. Learn from your mistakes and forge ahead. God can take your mess and make it a blessing. He is able. He will do it. He is faithful because Christ is in you. Don't ever limit yourself. Don't stop yourself either. There are great potentials within you. There are great apostles and pastors, evangelists and missionaries reading this book right now. That seed is within you. How you till it and keep it and give substance to it determines what the future will be. It is time to work out the Christ within.

When God made man in His own image and likeness the

law and commandment was for fruitfulness but Satan came and corrupted that image. Jesus is the express image of the father and He came to show us what we look like in the spirit.

Because as Christ is so are we in this world. And as the father has sent Him so he sends us. We must take the initiative. We must be bold and courageous.

Our initiatives must never be based on pride but on a sound understanding of the seed of God within us that must become fruitful.

Oh! how big, how great, how fruitful, how powerful is the Christ within you. If you can catch a glimpse of the image of Jesus within you and the seed of fruitfulness and greatness that God has planted, you will not be tossed to and fro by the issues of life.

I remember an incident while I was serving as a missionary in Kampala, Uganda. I was in a school run by an Indian gentleman. I was trying to get admission for my son. When I entered the headmaster's office he shouted "get out!!" He spoke as if he was speaking to an animal.

I looked at him and smiled. I put my hand in my pocket and balanced firmly in front of him. I'm not a Ugandan. I did not consider myself a Nigerian. I saw myself as a heavenly citizen.
I told myself angrily "If this man talks to me like that

again, he's going to see another side of me." On hearing the man's bark all the other parents ran out and then the man slowly lifted up his head, put on his glasses, looked at me again and he stood up to greet and attend to me. You need an understanding that there is someone great inside you.

One night after a powerful praise and worship session I suddenly had a flat tyre. It was along a very lonely road in Douala Cameroon where I was also serving as a missionary.

Just as I stopped the car to change the tyre, I was suddenly surrounded by four hefty hooligans; two in front of me and two at the back. I quickly picked up the jack. The presence of God was very much with me. There was no trace of any fear in my heart and I commanded them to move away, asking them "Do you know who I am? Do you know who I am?" Off course they did not but I was drunk with the knowledge of who I am in Christ and the ever abiding presence of Jehovah Sabaoth; the Lord of the heavenly armies. They hesitated for a moment and suddenly, the same way they appeared, they disappeared into the dark.

Build your gifts. Many people spend their lives solving one problem or another at the expense of discovering who they are.

You can never be fruitful when you spend your life responding to circumstances. Fruitfulness in life is achieved by developing

and maintaining the gifts of God in you.

Many are reading this now and they have great potential to be used by God in manifesting the gifts of the Holy Spirit but they never develop any sensitivity to Him neither do they position themselves.

They are not interested in paying the price although the potential is there. It should be a blessing to the body of Christ but it never comes out because the Holy Spirit will force no man. The following testimony goes to prove that manifestation always exercise of God's gifts in our lives.

"During the last seminar in Kumba, South West Cameroon, we had to go and search for my friend's mother who had been mad on the streets for about 10 years and eventually brought her to church. She was very violent and made a lot of noise. Pastor Peter then laid hands on her, commanded peace and left his mantle on her head. This marked the end of that madness. By the time we got home she was completely sane. Sister Kabul Em.

The gifts of God are without repentance Romans 11:29. But it is our responsibility to define that gift within us and refine it. Except you look inwards your gifts and the treasures inside you will never flow outwards and upwards to glorify God. God put them there that they might glorify Him. But it takes digging in for treasures to come up. The more you dig in, the higher you go up.

There are many people who don't like themselves. If they

are dark in complexion they want to bleach and be light by all means. The short man wants to be tall. The fat woman wants to be thin. The slim wants to be fat. This is because people have not identified what God has put in them.

That spirit of dissatisfaction is a satanic spirit.

He blinds your eyes to what you have and makes you to be distracted with yourself. He makes you believe you are nothing and that you cannot make it.

But that is the devil's lie.

Jesus came to show us what we can be. He's our perfect example. Everything you are lacking, Jesus can supply. Every place you are weak, He will strengthen. Every way in which your vision had been trampled upon, it will be renewed and revitalised in Jesus' Name.

There is a seed of fruitfulness inside you. It is the beginning of treasures and abundance. Please explore it friend. Till it and keep it that it might yield the more abundant life that Jesus came to give.

If you are born again the gifts of God are already planted as a seed in your heart. That seed is Jesus.

However, if you are not born again until you make yourself available for God to plant that seed in you, you cannot partake of the harvest of fruitfulness.

Right now eternity stands before you. The gifts of God, the treasures of heaven, the riches of the glory in the person of Jesus Christ can be planted in your life right now, even as you read this book.

What you need more than anything is Jesus Christ to usher you into eternal fruitfulness.

Stretch forth your hand, open your heart and receive His word now. Please pray this prayer of confession with me:

Heavenly Father, I come to You in the name of Jesus Christ and I confess my sins against you. Father, I ask You to forgive me. I believe Jesus Christ died for my sins and resurrected from the dead for my justification. I open my heart today and I invite You Lord Jesus Christ to come into my heart. I receive You as my Lord and my Saviour. I will follow You and serve You. Thank You Lord Jesus for saving me.

Amen.

The Lord will bless you. The Lord will cause His face to shine upon you. May the Lord prosper you. Make every gift, every treasure within you find full expression in Jesus' mighty name.

Amen

www.ingramcontent.com/pod-product-compliance
Lightning Source LLC
Chambersburg PA
CBHW061507040426
42450CB00008B/1509